Parents, please note:

This book contains 3 levels of learning

Level 1: Kid basics in **black text**

Level 2: Active learning questions in **blue text**

Level 3: Advanced information in **purple text**

Glossary and **Drawing Activity** are located in the back

Sign up for free activity sheets at www.tinkertoddlers.com

· · · · · · · · · · · · · · · · · · ·

Dedicated to John Ngui,
Thank you for being a wonderful teacher and friend.

No part of this book is to be duplicated or commercialized without explicit permission from the publisher.

Registered trademark & copyright © 2020 by GenBeam, LLC.
Book, cover, and internal designs and illustration © 2020 by GenBeam, LLC.
Published in the United States by GenBeam, LLC.
All rights reserved.

Visit us on the Web! ▶ www.tinkertoddlers.com

Contact us! ▶ tinkertoddlerbooks@gmail.com

Tinker Toddlers supports early STEM learning.
STEM is an acronym for science, technology, engineering, and mathematics. We provide simple explanations about emerging STEM concepts to the littlest learners to help facilitate the absorption of complex details later in life.

Introducing STEM early has shown to improve aptitude in math,
reading, writing, and exploratory learning in a wide spectrum of topics.

Supervised Machine Learning!
for Kids

Dr. Dhoot

Hi, my name is Aria and this is my cat, Snow. I have many machines in my house. They do lots of different things.
*What machines do you see in this picture? What machines are in your house?

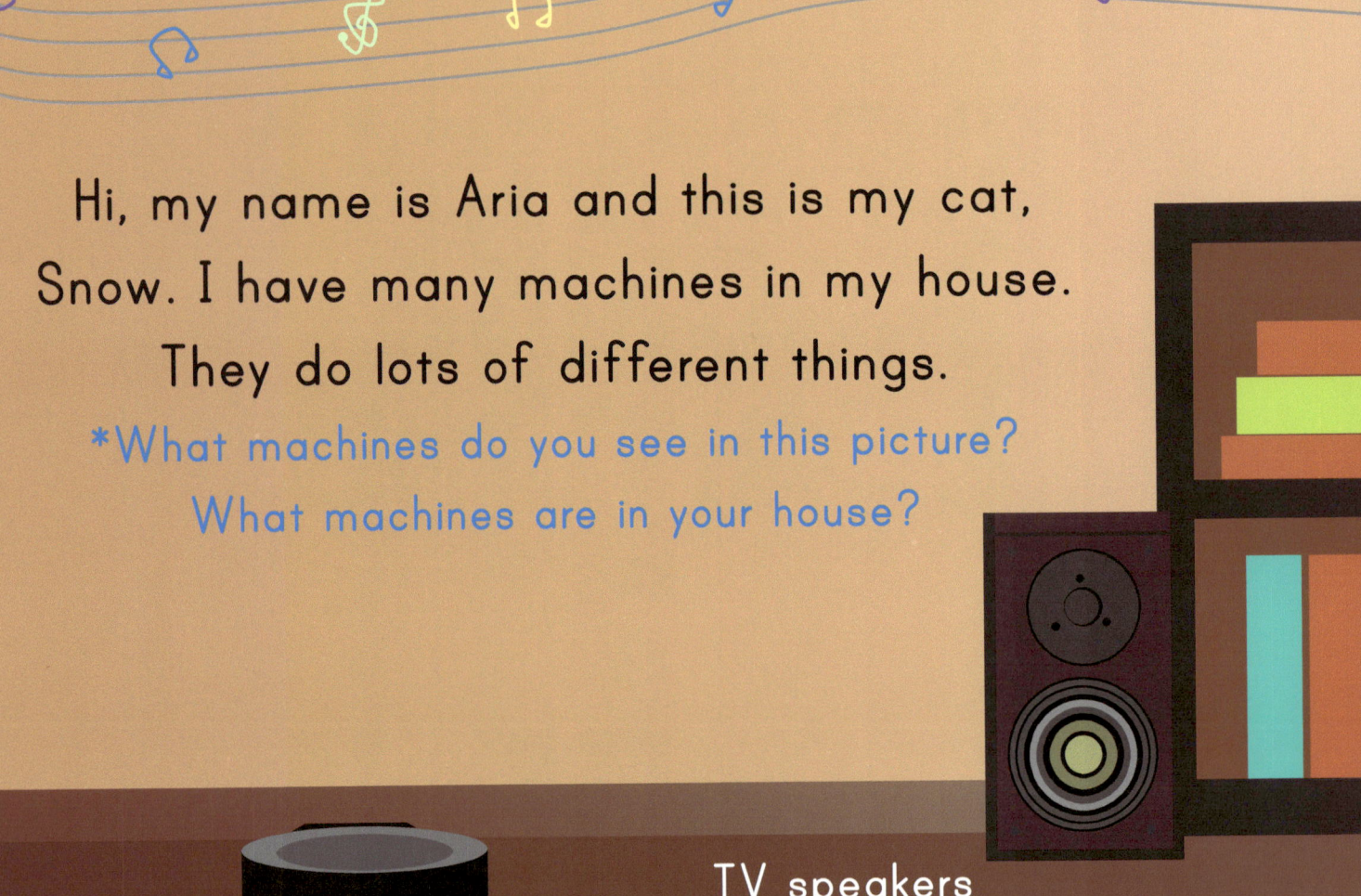

Vacuum

TV speakers

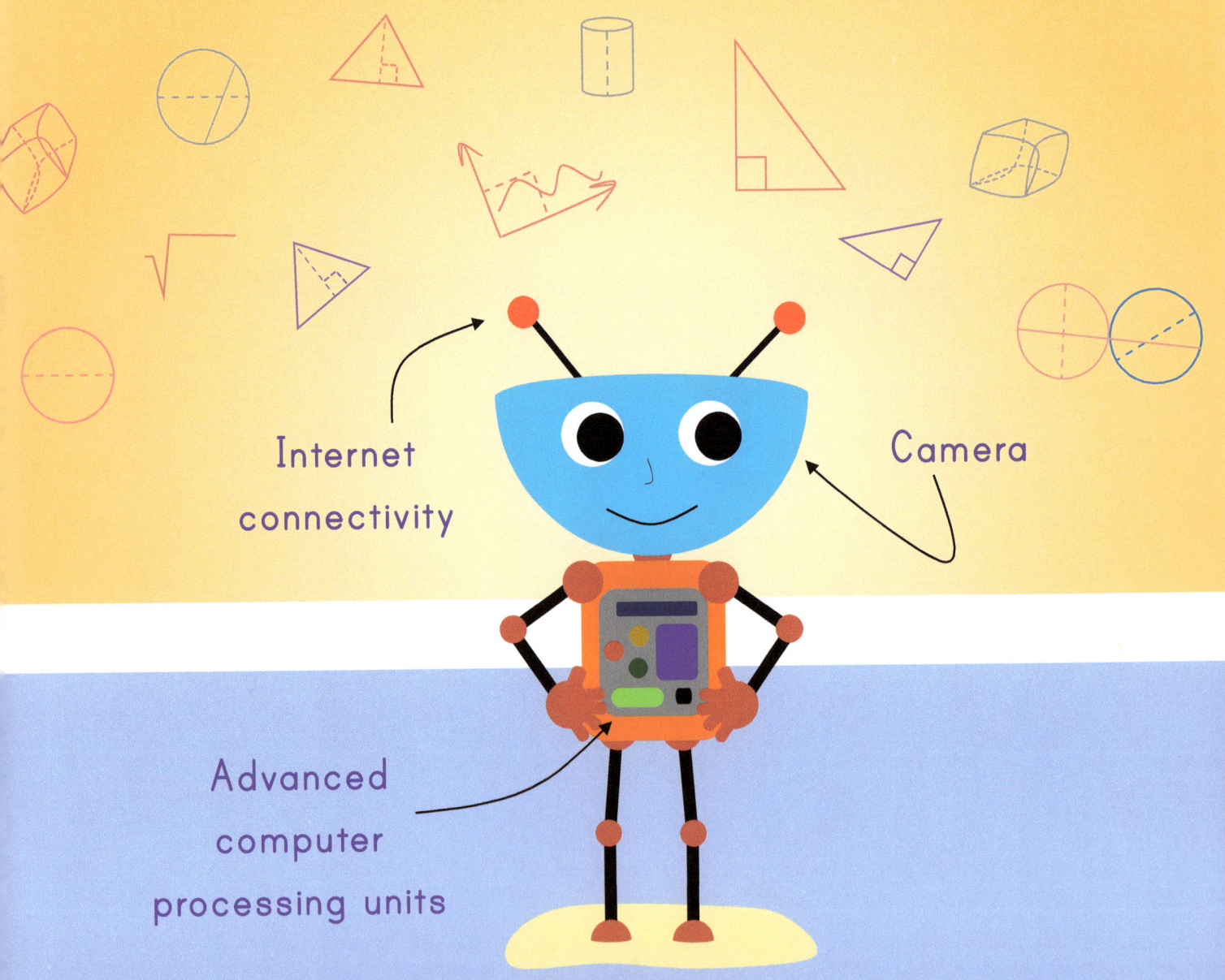

Dion has a superpower – he can learn, just like Snow and me.

Dion can learn with the help of a teacher.
In **Supervised Machine Learning**, a machine is told the right answer. To learn, Dion needs lots of examples (called **datasets**).

Dion can learn on its own.

In Unsupervised Machine Learning,
a machine is not told the right answer.

Today, we will help Dion learn about cats and dogs.

Let's teach Dion the difference between a cat and a dog.
Putting things into groups is called **classification**.

But, what makes a cat look different from a dog?

Dion will not learn if we are not specific.
Features are properties of what's being observed, like ear shape and nose size. Machines use these features to learn.

Dion can use a combination of details to tell between cats and dogs.

Dion follows a set of instructions, or an **algorithm**, to come to the right answer.

To learn, Dion practices, just like us.
The first set of examples is called a **training set**.
*What is circled in the pictures?
Dion uses these details to tell a cat from a dog.

Dion needs lots of practice.

To improve further learning, a second set of examples is used. This is called a **validation set**.

After all the practice, let's see if Dion has learned. Can it tell a cat from a dog?

The last set of examples is called a **test set**.

Now, Dion can tell a cat from a dog.

Teaching Dion to group cats and dogs was fun. We can teach Dion more things.

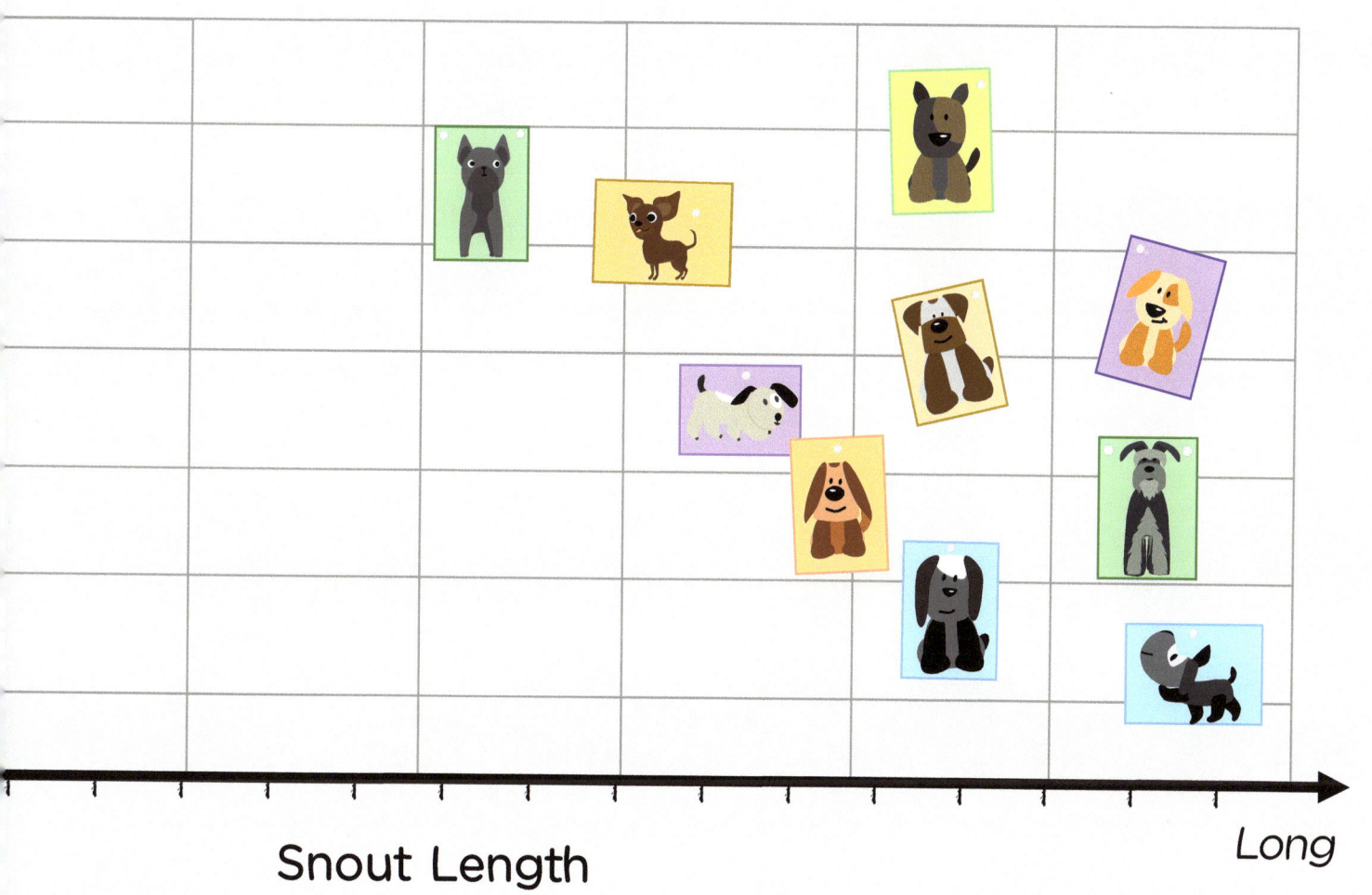

Snout Length

Long

With our help, Dion can learn relationships. For example, we can teach Dion to tell the relationship between height and weight.
This is called **regression analysis**.

Like before, Dion needs practice to learn the relationship between an animal's height and weight.

Dion needs a training set, validation set, and a test set to learn.

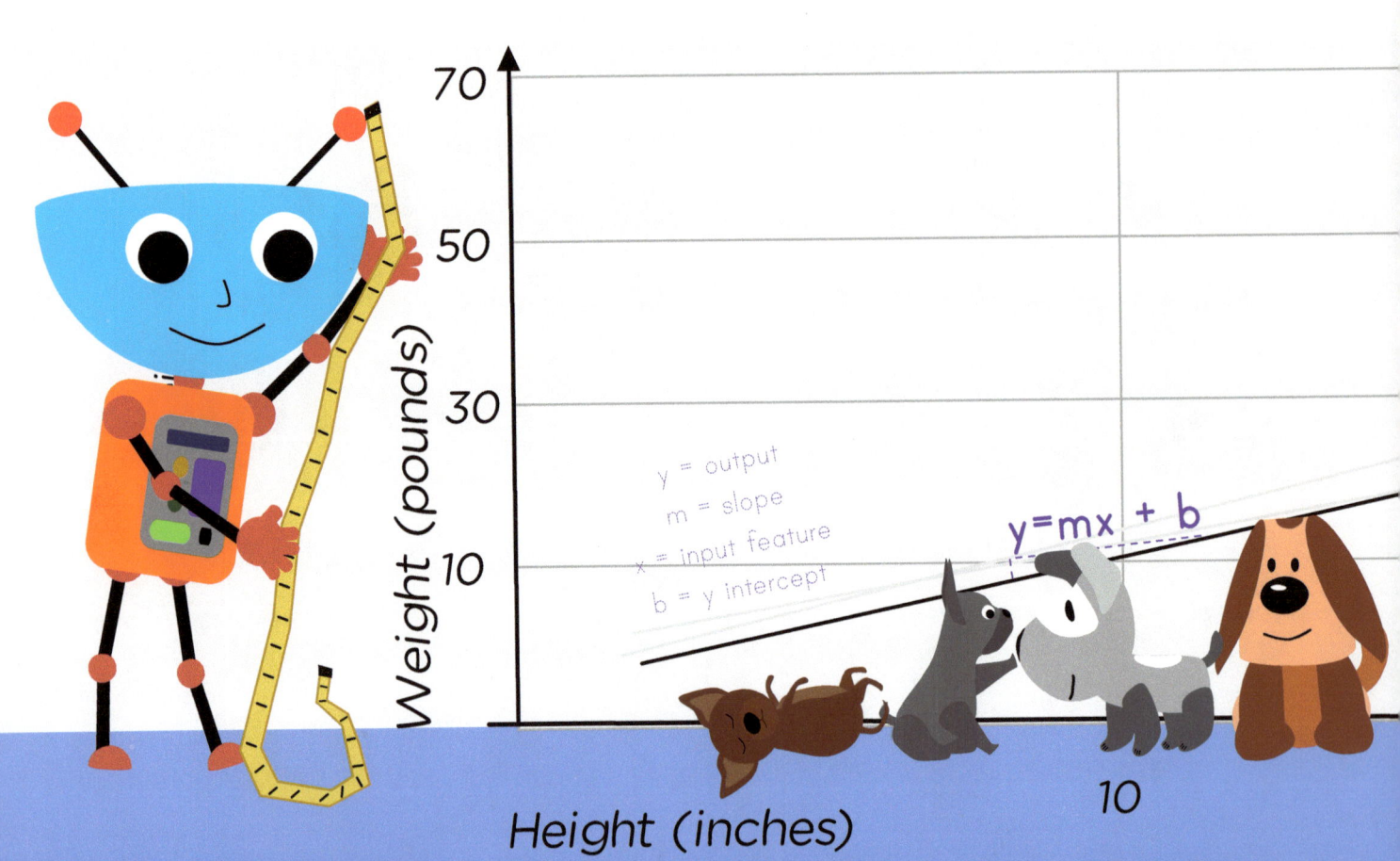

After all the practice, Dion learns animals that are taller, tend to be heavier.
*How much does the 10 inch puppy weigh?
*If a dog is 25 inches tall, can you predict its weight?

Dion isn't the only machine that can learn. Other machines in my house can learn too. My smart speaker learns my favorite songs.

*What's your favorite song?

Music streaming applications analyze the existing history of the listeners and recommend new songs.

We can teach machines to help outside the home too. Drones can learn to look out for dangers when making deliveries.

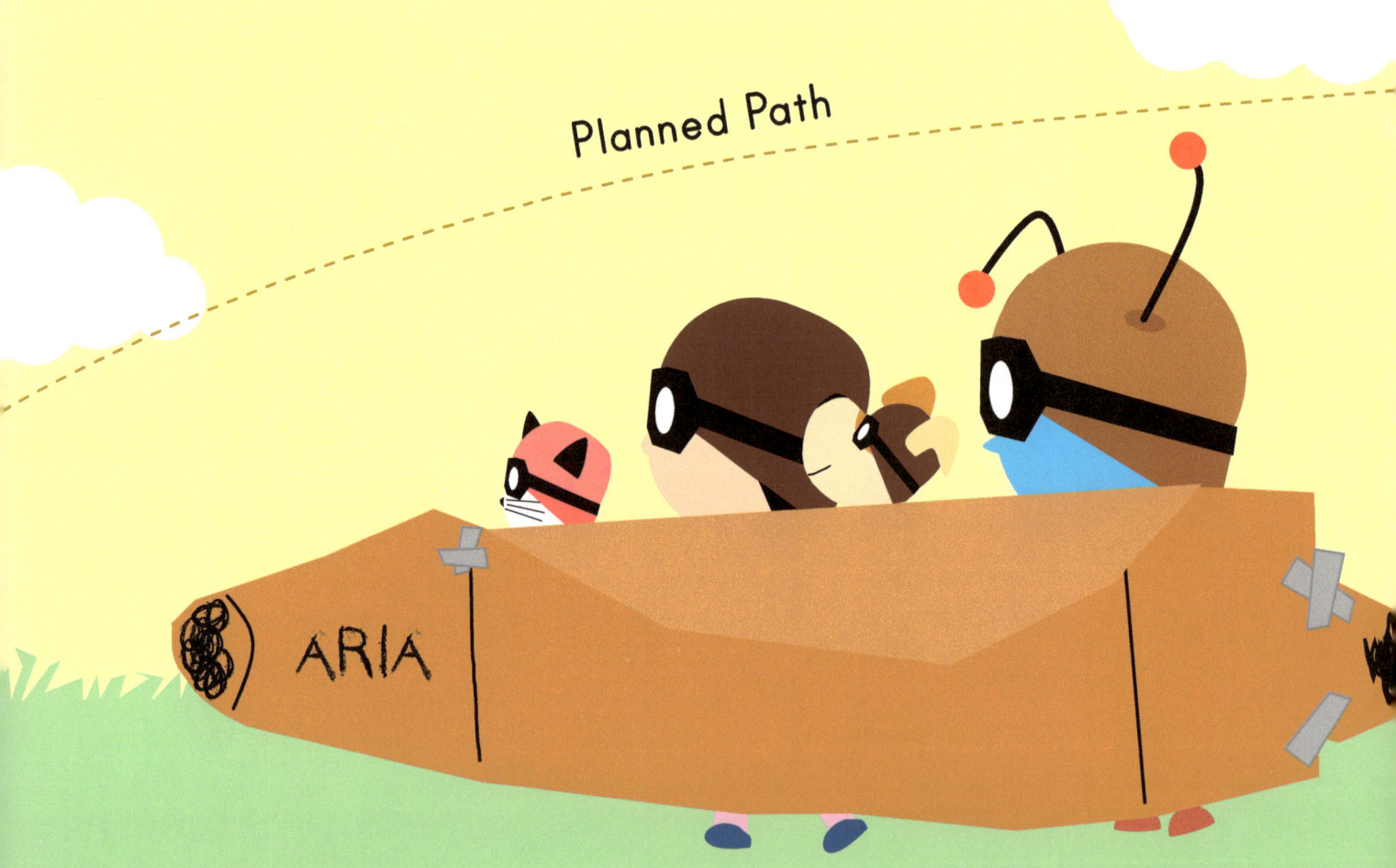

Dion is extraordinary!
When we teach machines like Dion,
they can do incredible things.

What do you want teach Dion?

Glossary

Algorithms are a list of steps that follows to complete a specific task.

Classification is a supervised machine learning approach in which the answer is categorized (e.g. car, bus, truck).

Datasets are lots and lots of examples that are used by machines to learn. There are different types of datasets (test set, training set, and validation set).

Features are properties or characteristics machines use to learn.

Regression Analysis is a supervised machine learning approach in which the answer is a specific value (ex: height, income, price, scores).

Supervised Machine Learning is a computer algorithm where we provide the right answer(s) to help the machine train.

Test Set is the final dataset of examples used to evaluate if the algorithm is working correctly.

Training Set is the initial dataset of examples used to train a machine to output the right answer. The training set is used to help the system learn.

Validation Set is the second dataset of examples used to train a machine to output the right answer. The validation set is used to improve the way the system learns.

Questions for your budding learner

Dion is extraordinary because he can learn.
If you had a machine that can learn, what would it look like, and what would you teach it? Draw a picture of your learning machine.

Dion learned to group cats and dogs and put them all on his wall.
Can you group these animals differently?
Here are some ideas: group by color, or by which ones are standing and which ones are walking.

Machines are everywhere.
What machines are around you?

Not all machines can learn.
Can you name three machines that can learn?
Can you name three machines that cannot learn?

Share your answers and learning machine picture by asking a grown-up to email us at tinkertoddlerbooks@gmail.com or by posting a review on Amazon!

My Learning Machine

Dear Reader,

I hope you enjoyed reading about supervised machine learning.

Science and technology are evolving rapidly, and it can be hard to keep up. I hope you and your little learner(s) enjoyed learning the very basics and continue to build your knowledge base.

If you liked this story and want to read more like it, there is a whole series of Tinker Toddlers books, just waiting for you.

Best,

Dr. Dhoot

Tinker Toddlers®

www.TinkerToddlers.com

tinkertoddlerbooks@gmail.com

Tinker Toddlers' Growing Library

 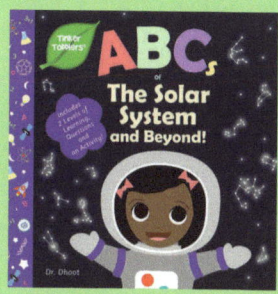 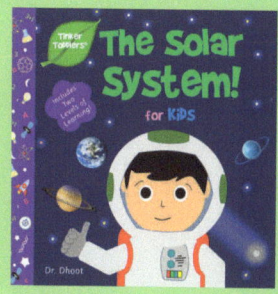

  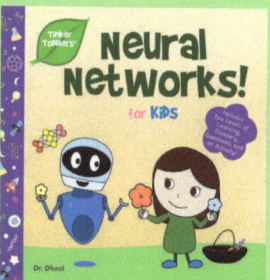 

amazon.com/author/drdhoot

tinkertoddlerbooks@gmail.com

Special thanks to AI for K-12 educators
for their contributions in reviewing this book.

To support our efforts, please leave a review.

<u>Tinker Toddler books are now available in your local library!</u>
If your library does not carry them yet, simply request
they do (eBooks or print). Libraries appreciate hearing
from their communities.

www.ingramcontent.com/pod-product-compliance
Lightning Source LLC
Chambersburg PA
CBHW040027050426
42453CB00002B/28